SEP 2 6 2006

P9-ECR-896

Frankie and Johnny in the Clair De Lune

Frankie and Johnny in the Clair De Lune

by
TERRENCE MCNALLY

The Fireside Theatre
Garden City, New York

For Maurine McElroy

FRANKIE AND JOHNNY IN THE CLAIR DE LUNE was first produced by Manhattan Theatre Club Stage II at City Center in New York City on June 2nd 1987, with the following cast:

FRANKIE	Kathy Bates
JOHNNY	F. Murray Abraham
VOICE OF RADIO AN-NOUNCER	Dominic Cuskern

It transferred to Manhattan Theatre Club Stage 1 at City Center on October 14th 1987, with the following cast:

FRANKIE	Kathy Bates
JOHNNY	Kenneth Welsh
VOICE OF RADIO AN-NOUNCER	Dominic Cuskern

Both productions were directed by Paul Benedict. Sets by James Noone. Costumes by David Woolard. Lighting by David Noling. Sound by John Gromada. The Production Stage Manager was Pamela Singer.

This production transferred to the Westside Arts Theatre in New York City on December 4th 1987. It was produced by Steven Baruch, Thomas Viertel, Richard Frankel and Jujamcyn Theaters/Margo Lion.

Frankie and Johnny
in the
Clair De Lune

TIME

The present.

PLACE

New York City.

SETTING

FRANKIE's one-room apartment in a walk-up tenement in the West Fifties. The fourth wall looks onto the backyard and the apartments behind. When the sofa bed is down, as it is for much of the play, the room is quite cramped.

CHARACTERS

FRANKIE   Striking but not conventional good looks. She has a sense of humor and a fairly tough exterior. She is also frightened and can be very hard to reach.

JOHNNY   JOHNNY's best feature is his personality. He works at it. He is in good physical condition.

VOICE OF RADIO ANNOUNCER

ACT I

ACT I

AT RISE: *Darkness. We hear the sounds of a man and woman making love. They are getting ready to climax. The sounds they are making are noisy, ecstatic and familiar. Above all, they must be graphic. The intention is a portrait in sound of a passionate man and woman making love and reaching climax together.*

The real thing.

They come.

Silence. Heavy breathing. We become aware that the radio has been playing Bach's Goldberg Variations *in the piano version.*

By this point, the curtain has been up for at least two minutes. No light, no dialogue, just the sounds of lovemaking and now the Bach.

FRANKIE: God, I wish I still smoked. Life used to be so much more fun. *(JOHNNY laughs softly)* What?

JOHNNY: Nothing. *(He laughs again, a little louder)* Oh, God!

FRANKIE: Well, it must be something!

JOHNNY: It's dumb, it's gross, it's stupid, it's . . . *(He howls with laughter)* I'm sorry. Jesus, this is terrible. I don't know what's gotten into me. I'll be all right. *(He catches his breath. FRANKIE turns on a bedside lamp)* Really, I'm sorry. It has nothing to do with you.

FRANKIE: Are you okay now?

JOHNNY: Yes. No! *(He bursts into laughter again. And now* FRANKIE *bursts into laughter: a wild, uncontrollable, infectious sound)* What are you laughing at?

FRANKIE: I don't know!

(Now they are both laughing hilariously. It is the kind of laughter that gets out of control and people have trouble breathing. FRANKIE *rolls off the bed and lands on the floor with a slight thud)*

JOHNNY: Are you okay?

FRANKIE: No!

(Now it is FRANKIE *who is laughing solo. It is a wonderfully joyful sound: a lot of stored-up feeling is being released)*

JOHNNY: Should I get you something?

FRANKIE: Yes! My mother!

JOHNNY: A beer, a Coke, anything?

FRANKIE: A bag to put over my head!

JOHNNY: You really want your mother?

FRANKIE: Are you crazy?

JOHNNY: You have the most . . . the most wonderful breasts.

FRANKIE: Thank you. *(She bursts into new laughter. This time* JOHNNY*doesn't join in at all. Eventually they are both still. They listen to the Bach in silence and without moving)* That's nice music. Very . . . I want to say "chaste."

JOHNNY: I'll tell you why I was laughing. All of a sudden—just like that!—I remembered this time back in high school when I was making out with this really beautiful girl and was feeling incredibly suave and sophisticated and wondering if anybody would believe my good fortune and worrying if she was going to let me go all the way—I think it would have been her first time too—when all of a sudden I let out this incredibly loud fart. Like that. Only louder. It was awful. *(he laughs again)* And there was no pretending it wasn't me. You couldn't say something like "Boy, did you hear that thunder?" or "Jesus, Peggy was that you?" The best I could come up with was "May I use your bathroom?" which only made it worse. And there in the bathroom was her mother taking a bath at ten o'clock at night. She had one arm up, washing her armpit. I said something real cool like, "Hello Mrs. Roberts." She screamed and I ran out of the house. I tripped over the garbage cans and tore my pants climbing over the backyard fence. I must've run twenty blocks, most of them with dogs chasing me. I thought my life was over. We never mentioned what happened and I never dated her again and I lost my virginity with someone else. But why that fart banged back into my consciousness just then . . . !

FRANKIE: Could we change the subject?

JOHNNY: What's the matter?

FRANKIE: I'm not a prude . . .

JOHNNY: I know that! Any woman who . . .

FRANKIE: I just . . . we all draw the line somewhere.

JOHNNY: And with you it's farts?

FRANKIE: Is that going to be a problem?

JOHNNY: You don't think any kind of farting is funny?

FRANKIE: Not off the top of my head I don't.

JOHNNY: Hunh! I always have. I don't know why I find a lot of things funny. Like Corgies.

FRANKIE: Corgies?

JOHNNY: You know the dogs the Queen of England has?

FRANKIE: No.

JOHNNY: Sure you do. They're about this big, tan and look like walking heads. Everytime I see one, I get hysterical. Show me a Corgie and I'm yours.

FRANKIE: I guess a farting Corgie would really lay you out!

JOHNNY: See? You do have a sense of humor about it!

(They both laugh. Then silence. The Bach plays on)

FRANKIE: You know what I mean? About the music? It's pure.

JOHNNY: Did you come?

FRANKIE: No one's that good at faking it.

JOHNNY: I thought so. Good. I'm glad.

FRANKIE: There! Hear that? It makes me think of . . . grace.

JOHNNY: You mean, the thing it's good to be in the state of?

FRANKIE: The movement kind. You know . . . *(She moves her arm in a flowing gesture and sways her shoulders to the music)* Flowing.

JOHNNY: So why were you laughing?

FRANKIE: I don't know. Because you were, I guess. You sounded so happy. Little did I know!

JOHNNY: I *was* happy. I'm still happy. Where are you going?

FRANKIE: Nowhere.

JOHNNY: You're going somewhere.

FRANKIE: The closet.

JOHNNY: Why?

FRANKIE: A robe.

JOHNNY: You don't need a—

FRANKIE: I'm cold.

JOHNNY: I want to bask in your nakedness.

FRANKIE: Sure you do.

(FRANKIE turns on the overhead room light)

JOHNNY: Ow!

FRANKIE: I'm sorry, I'm sorry!

(She turns off the overhead light. The first quick impression we have of the room is that it is modest and not especially tidy)

JOHNNY: Warn somebody when you're going to do that! I hate bright lights but especially right after making love. Talk about a mood changer! Besides,

I think you see the other person better in the light of the afterglow. *(Pause)* Did you hear what I just said?

FRANKIE: Yes.

JOHNNY: Just checking.

(While FRANKIE *gets a robe out of the closet,* JOHNNY *goes through her purse on the bedtable until he finds a pair of sunglasses)*

FRANKIE: Remember when everybody used to light up the second it seemed they were through making love? "I'm coming, I'm coming, I came. You got a match?"

JOHNNY: I didn't smoke.

FRANKIE: Never?

JOHNNY: Ever.

FRANKIE: You've got a smoker's personality.

JOHNNY: That's what they tell me.

FRANKIE: I just made that up.

JOHNNY: So did I. And I didn't like women who did.

FRANKIE: Did what? Smoked? Then you would have hated me. Marla the Human Furnace.

JOHNNY: Marla? I thought your name was Francis.

FRANKIE: It is, it is! Don't panic. I just made that up, too. I don't know where it came from. From what Freudian depth it sprung.

JOHNNY: Marla! Ecchh!

FRANKIE: You put too much stock in this name business, John.

(She comes back to bed wearing a bathrobe. JOHNNY *looks fairly ridiculous in her sunglasses)*

JOHNNY: It's Johnny, please.

FRANKIE: Are those mine? I wish you'd stay out of my—

JOHNNY: I hate John.

FRANKIE: Did you hear me?

JOHNNY: I heard you.

FRANKIE: I wish you'd act like you heard me.

JOHNNY: May I wear your sunglasses?

FRANKIE: Yes.

JOHNNY: Thank you. God, you're beautiful. Are you coming back to bed?

FRANKIE: I don't know.

JOHNNY: John sounds like a toilet or a profession. And Jack only works if you're a Kennedy or a Nicholson.

FRANKIE: I read somewhere there are millions of young people, a whole generation, who don't have a clue who John Kennedy was. Do you believe it? To me, he was only yesterday. I love Jack Nicholson. Did you see *Prizzi's Honor?*

JOHNNY: Six times.

FRANKIE: Six times?

JOHNNY: The first time I popped for it, six bucks, the good old days, remember them? Seven bucks gets my goat, don't get me started! Then five on VCR, you know a rental, when I was getting over my hernia and I couldn't get out of bed so hot.

FRANKIE: You've got a VCR?

JOHNNY: Oh sure. Stereo TV, VCR. I'm working on a dish.

FRANKIE: And you've got a hernia?

JOHNNY: Had, had. Here, I'll show you.

FRANKIE: Wow. That's big. Did it hurt?

JOHNNY: *Comme ci, comme ça.* You got any scars?

FRANKIE: Everybody has scars.

JOHNNY: Where? I'll just look.

FRANKIE: No.

JOHNNY: Okay, okay. You know, they filmed it right near where I live.

FRANKIE: *Prizzi's Honor?*

JOHNNY: Oh sure.

FRANKIE: In Brooklyn?

JOHNNY: Brooklyn Heights. Please, don't get us confused with the rest of the borough. Would you like it if I referred to your neighborhood as Chinatown?

FRANKIE: Fifty-third and Tenth?

JOHNNY: Anyway! You know the house that guy lived in, the one with the funny voice? Hinley or something? He got nominated for an Oscar or something but I don't think he won. Or maybe he did.

FRANKIE: The one who played the Don?

JOHNNY: That's the one. Headley, Henkley, Hinley.

FRANKIE: You live in that house?

JOHNNY: No, but I can see their roof from my bathroom window.

FRANKIE: Oh.

JOHNNY: You know what those movie stars get when they're on location like that? Their own trailers with their name on the door. Big long trailers. Not like the kind you see in Montauk, those ugly little Airstream jobbies. At least I think they're ugly. No, these are the big long kind like you see sitting up on blocks in a trailer park that people live in full time, people who aren't going anywhere in 'em they're so big! I'm talking trailers with bedrooms and bathtubs. I'm talking major mobile homes.

FRANKIE: I hate trailers.

JOHNNY: So do I. That's not the point.

FRANKIE: I'd rather die than live in a trailer. The very words "mobile home" strike me with such terror.

JOHNNY: I believe I had the floor.

FRANKIE: Who the hell wants a living room that moves, for Christ's sake? Ecch! Sorry.

JOHNNY: Anyway, they each have their own trailer. I mean, Jack Nicholson is on one side of the street in his block-long trailer and Kathleen Turner is on the other in hers.

FRANKIE: I'm sorry but I don't get her message.

JOHNNY: Will you let me finish?

FRANKIE: Do you?

JOHNNY: Yes, but that's not the point either. They also give these trailers to people you never even heard of, like this Hinley, Headley, Hinckley, what's-his-face character.

FRANKIE: Is that the point?

JOHNNY: I'm not saying he's not a good actor but his own trailer? I'm in the wrong business.

FRANKIE: We both are.

JOHNNY: Do you think I talk too much?

FRANKIE: I don't think you always give the other person a chance to—

JOHNNY: That's what my best friend says. "I talk because I got a lot to say, Ernie," I tell him but he doesn't seem to understand that. Talking to you comes real easy. I appreciate that. And I won't pretend I wasn't looking forward to this evening.

FRANKIE: Well, it's been very . . .

JOHNNY: What do you mean, "been"? It still is. "The night is young, the stars are clear and if you care to go walking, dear." I admit I love the sound of my own voice. So shoot me, give me the electric chair, it ain't over till the fat lady sings. Can I have a beer?

FRANKIE: I'm sorry.

JOHNNY: You say that too much.

(He goes to refrigerator as FRANKIE *crosses to floor lamp by easy chair and turns it on)*

FRANKIE: Is this okay? I hate gloom.

JOHNNY: Light like this is fine. It's the harsh blinding kind I can't stand. Now where are you going?

FRANKIE: Just in here. *(She goes to bathroom door, opens it, turns on light, goes in, leaving door open so that more light spills into the room)* Keep talking. I can hear you.

JOHNNY: You mean about the light? There are some delicatessens I just won't go into, they're so bright. There's one over on Madison Avenue and Twenty-eighth Street that is so bright from the overhead fluorescents that you wouldn't believe it. I complained. I don't even shop there and I complained. "What are you trying to do? Get an airplane to land in here?" They just looked at me like I was an idiot. Of course, I doubt if they even spoke English. Most Koreans don't. It's getting to the point where you can count on one hand the number of people who speak English in this city. *(He goes to bathroom door and stands watching* FRANKIE *within)* Look, I know I talk too much. It's just that certain things get my goat. Things like ninety-foot trailers for people I never heard of . . . *(*FRANKIE *comes out of the bathroom. She has changed into a brightly*

*colored kimono. She has a hairbrush in her hand
and will brush her hair during the following)* Hi
there.

FRANKIE: Hello.

JOHNNY: . . . waste, especially water—you got a
leaky faucet around here? Lady, I'm your plumber
—and the fact this is supposed to be an English-
speaking nation only nobody speaks English anymore. Other than that, I'm cool and I'll shut up
now and won't say another word. I'm locking my
mouth and throwing away the key.

(He watches FRANKIE *comb her hair)*

FRANKIE: Did you get Easter off? *(*JOHNNY *shakes his
head)* Neither did I. And watch us twiddle our
thumbs. Last Easter you could've shot moose in
there. Forget tips. I've already decided, I'm gonna
call in sick. Life's too short, you know? You want
some juice? It's home-made. I mean, I squeezed it
myself. That's right, you're working on a beer. I'd
offer you a joint but I don't do that anymore. Not
that I think other people shouldn't. It's just that I
can't personally handle it anymore. I mean, I
didn't like what it was doing to me. I mean, the
bottom line is: it isn't good for you. For me, I mean.
It isn't good for me. Hey, come on, don't!

JOHNNY: Can I say one more thing?

FRANKIE: I wish you would.

JOHNNY: I could watch you do that for maybe the rest of my life.

FRANKIE: Get real.

JOHNNY: I think a woman combing and fixing her hair is one of the supremely great sights of life. I'd put it up there with the Grand Canyon and a mother nursing her child. Triumphant facts of nature. That's all. Now I'm locking my eyes shut and throwing away the key. *(He closes his eyes)*

FRANKIE: What am I supposed to do?

JOHNNY: Sshh, pretend you can't hear. Next thing she'll want is your ears.

FRANKIE: Oh my God, it's three o'clock! Look, I'd ask you to stay over but . . . I don't know about you but I'm kind of drained, you know? I mean, that was pretty intense back there. Harrowing. No, not harrowing, that doesn't sound right. I'm too pooped to pop, all right? Oh come on, you know what I mean!

(JOHNNY inhales very slowly and very deeply)

JOHNNY: She's wearing something new. This part is called Scent Torture. I love it, I love it!

FRANKIE: You know, you're a very intense person. One minute you're making love like somebody just let you out of jail and the next you're telling me watching me brush my hair is like the Grand Canyon. Very intense or very crazy. Look, I'm glad what happened happened. If we both play our cards right, maybe it will happen again . . . Hello?

JOHNNY: I hear you.

FRANKIE: I wish you'd open your eyes.

(JOHNNY *very slowly opens his eyes and turns to face* FRANKIE. *He reacts as if blinded*)

JOHNNY: Aaaagggg! It's worse than the delicatessen! Such blinding beauty!

FRANKIE: I'm serious.

(JOHNNY *stops screaming and looks at her again*)

JOHNNY: *(Quietly)* So am I.

FRANKIE: That's exactly what I mean. One minute you're kidding and the next you're looking at me like that.

JOHNNY: Like what?

FRANKIE: Like that! People don't go around looking at one another like that. It's too intense. You don't look, you stare. It gives me the creeps. I suppose it's very flattering but it's not something I feel real comfortable with. It's like if you would send me a million roses, I'd be impressed but I wouldn't know where to put them. I don't need a million roses.

One would be just fine. So if you just looked at me *occasionally* in the future like that. Look, obviously I like you. I like you a lot. What's the matter?

JOHNNY: I'm just drinking all this in.

FRANKIE: You're not the easiest person to talk to anybody ever met.

JOHNNY: I certainly hope not. How old are you?

FRANKIE: None of your business. How old are you?

JOHNNY: What do you think?

FRANKIE: Midforties.

JOHNNY: Ouch!

FRANKIE: Maybe late thirties.

JOHNNY: I can live with that.

FRANKIE: Come on, how old are you?

JOHNNY: I don't know.

FRANKIE: Everybody knows how old they are.

JOHNNY: I used to, then I forgot.

FRANKIE: That's a great answer. Can I borrow it?

JOHNNY: I did.

FRANKIE: Who from?

JOHNNY: Some old lady on the Carson show? I don't remember. Half the things I got up here, I don't remember where they came from. It doesn't seem fair. People ought to get credit for all the things they give and teach us. You're fabulous.

FRANKIE: I feel like I'm supposed to say "thank you."

JOHNNY: It's not necessary.

FRANKIE: Instead, I want to ask you to quit sneaking up on me like that. We're talking about one thing, people who teach, and wham! you slip in there with some kind of intimate, personal remark. I like being told I'm fabulous. Who wouldn't? I'd like some warning first, that's all. This is not a spontaneous person you have before you.

JOHNNY: You're telling me that wasn't spontaneous?

FRANKIE: That was different. I'm talking about the larger framework of things. What people are doing in your life. What they're doing in your bed is easy or at least it used to be back before we had to start checking each other out. I don't know about you but I get so sick and tired of living this way, that we're gonna die from one another, that every so often I just want to act like Saturday night really is a Saturday night, the way they used to be.

JOHNNY: I'm very glad we had this Saturday night.

FRANKIE: I never would have said that if I knew you better.

JOHNNY: How well do you want to know me?

FRANKIE: I'll let you know Monday between orders. "I got a BLT down working!" "Tell me about your childhood." "Take the moo out of two!" "Were you toilet trained?"

JOHNNY: Come here.

FRANKIE: Are you sure you don't want something before you go?

JOHNNY: Come here.

FRANKIE: I've got some meatloaf in the fridge.

JOHNNY: Come here.

(FRANKIE *moves a few steps toward* JOHNNY, *who is sitting on the edge of the bed*)

FRANKIE: What?

JOHNNY: Closer.

(FRANKIE *moves closer to* JOHNNY, *who pulls her all the way toward him and buries his face in her middle*)

FRANKIE: I can toast some bread. Butter and catsup. A cold meatloaf sandwich. All the way back to Brooklyn . . .

JOHNNY: Heights.

FRANKIE: Heights! This time of night. Aren't you hungry?

JOHNNY: I'm starving.

FRANKIE: No!

JOHNNY: Why not?

FRANKIE: We just did.

JOHNNY: So?

FRANKIE: I can't.

JOHNNY: What do you mean, you can't?

FRANKIE: I don't want to. (JOHNNY *immediately stops nuzzling* FRANKIE. *Both hands fly up with palms outward*) You don't have to take it like that. I'm sorry. Just not right now. You know, you're right: I do say "I'm sorry" a lot around you. There's something about you that makes me feel like I'm letting you down all the time. Like you have all these expectations of me that I can't fulfill. I'm sorry—there I go again!—but what you see here is what you get. I am someone who likes to eat after making love and right now I feel like a cold meat loaf sandwich on white toast with butter and catsup with a large glass of very cold milk and I wish you would stop looking at me like that.

JOHNNY: Open your robe.

FRANKIE: No. Why?

JOHNNY: I want to look at your pussy.

FRANKIE: No. Why?

JOHNNY: It's beautiful.

FRANKIE: It is not. You're just saying that.

JOHNNY: I think it is. I'm telling you, you have a beautiful pussy—!

FRANKIE: I hate that word, Johnny!

JOHNNY: —all right, thing! And I'm asking you to open your robe so I can look at it. Just look. Fifteen seconds. You can time me. Then you can make *two* cold meat loaf sandwiches and *two* big glasses of milk. Just hold the catsup on one.

FRANKIE: I don't know if you're playing games or being serious.

JOHNNY: Both. Serious games. Do you have to name everything? If I had said, "You have a beautiful parakeet," you'd have let me see it and we'd be eating those sandwiches already.

FRANKIE: I had a parakeet. I hated it. I was glad when it died. *(She opens her robe)* Okay?

JOHNNY: Oh! Yes!

FRANKIE: *(Continuing to hold her robe open as* JOHNNY *sits on edge of bed and looks)* I'm timing this! I told my cousin I didn't want a bird. I hate birds. She swore I'd love a parakeet. What's to love? *(She almost drops the robe)* They don't do anything except not sing when you want them to, sing when you don't and make those awful scratching noises on that awful sandpaper on the floor of their cell. I mean cage! If I ever have another pet it'll be a dog. A Golden Lab. Something that shows a little enthusiasm when you walk through the door. Something you can hold. The only time I got my hands on that goddamn parakeet was the day it dropped dead and I had to pick it up to throw it in the garbage can. Hey, come on! This has gotta be fifteen seconds. *(*FRANKIE *closes her robe.* JOHNNY *takes her hand, kisses it, rubs his cheek against it.* FRANKIE *stands awkwardly)* You really would like a sandwich?

JOHNNY: But no catsup.

FRANKIE: Catsup's what makes a cold meat loaf sandwich good.

JOHNNY: I'm allergic. Catsup and peaches.

FRANKIE: Ugh!

JOHNNY: Well, not in the same dish! *(He is still nuzzling her fingers)*

FRANKIE: Can I have my hand back?

JOHNNY: Do you want it back?

FRANKIE: Well, you want a sandwich, don't you?

JOHNNY: I want you to notice how we're connecting. My hand is flowing into yours. My eyes are trying to see inside yours.

FRANKIE: That's not connecting. That's holding and staring. Connecting is when the other person isn't even around and you could die from just thinking of them.

JOHNNY: That's missing. This is connecting.

FRANKIE: Yeah, well, it ain't how a sandwich gets made. *(She takes her hand from* JOHNNY *and goes to kitchen area of the apartment, where she takes out all the makings of her meat loaf sandwich and begins to prepare them.* JOHNNY *will just watch her from his place on the bed)* My father used to say a good meat loaf and gravy with mashed potatoes was food fit for the gods.

JOHNNY: You're kidding! That's exactly what my old man used to say.

FRANKIE: Of course, considering our family budget we didn't have too many other options. Guess what, Pop? I still don't. *(She laughs.* JOHNNY *laughs with her)* You want to turn on the television?

JOHNNY: Why?

FRANKIE: We don't have to watch it. You know, just sound. I do it all the time. Company. It beats a parakeet.

JOHNNY: I'd rather watch you.

FRANKIE: Do you ever watch the Channel 5 Movie Club on Saturday night? That's right, you got a VCR. They have this thing called the Movie Club. Talk about dumb gimmicks. You put your name and address on a postcard. If they draw it, you go on the air and tell everybody what your favorite movie is and they show it, along with intermission breaks where they tell you certain little-known facts about the movie I just as soon wouldn't have known, such as "Susan Hayward was already stricken with a fatal cancer when she made this sparkling comedy." Kind of puts a pall on things, you know?

JOHNNY: I was on that program.

FRANKIE: You were not.

JOHNNY: Sure I was.

FRANKIE: What was your favorite movie?

JOHNNY: I forget.

FRANKIE: You probably don't even have one.

(JOHNNY *has gotten up off the bed and come over to*
where FRANKIE *is working. He finds a place to sit*
very close to where she stands making the sand-
wiches)

JOHNNY: You know what I was thinking while I was
looking at you over there?

FRANKIE: I should have guessed this was coming!

JOHNNY: I was thinking, "There's got to be more to
life than this," but at times like this I'll be god-
damned if I know what it is.

FRANKIE: You don't give up, do you?

JOHNNY: I want to drown in this woman. I want to die
here. So why is she talking about parakeets and
meat loaf? The inequity of human relationships! I
actually thought that word: "inequity." I didn't
even know it was in my vocabulary. And what's
that other one? "Disparity!" Yeah, that's it. The
disparity between us at that moment. I mean,
there I was, celebrating you, feasting on your love-
liness, and you were talking about a fucking, pardon my French, parakeet!

FRANKIE: Maybe it's because I was ill at ease.

JOHNNY: Because of me?

FRANKIE: Maybe I don't like being looked at down
there that way how the hell should I know?

JOHNNY: Bullshit! You don't like being looked at, period.

FRANKIE: Ow!

JOHNNY: What happened?

FRANKIE: I cut myself.

JOHNNY: Let me see.

FRANKIE: It's all right.

JOHNNY: Let me see. *(He sucks the blood from her finger)*

FRANKIE: Look, I don't think this is going to work out. It was very nice while it lasted but like I said . . .

JOHNNY: You'll live. *(He releases her hand)*

FRANKIE: . . . I'm a BLT down sort of person and I think you're looking for someone a little more pheasant under glass. Where are you going?

JOHNNY: I'll get a bandage.

FRANKIE: That's okay.

JOHNNY: No problem.

FRANKIE: Really. What are you doing?

(JOHNNY has gone into the bathroom. We hear him

going through the medicine cabinet looking for a
bandage as he continues to speak through the open
door)

JOHNNY: I don't remember you saying you were a
BLT down sort of person.

FRANKIE: I thought I implied it when I was talking
about the meat loaf.

(JOHNNY comes out of the bathroom with a box of
Band-Aids and a bottle of iodine)

JOHNNY: It's because I said you had a beautiful pussy,
isn't it? Give me your finger.

(FRANKIE holds out her finger while JOHNNY disin-
fects and dresses it)

FRANKIE: It's because you said a lot of things. Ow!

JOHNNY: A man compliments a woman. All right,
maybe he uses street talk but it's nice street talk,
affectionate. It's not one of them ugly words, like
the one I'm sure we're both familiar with, the one
that begins with *c.* I didn't say you had a beautiful
c. I was saying something loving and you took of-
fense.

FRANKIE: I told you I wasn't very spontaneous!

JOHNNY: Boy, if you had said to me, "Johnny, you
have the most terrific dick on you," I would be so

happy. *(He finishes with the Band-Aids)* There you go.

FRANKIE: Thank you.

JOHNNY: You want to see scarred fingers! *(He holds up his hands to* FRANKIE*)*

FRANKIE: *(Wincing at the sight)* Please!

JOHNNY: They don't hurt.

FRANKIE: I don't want to look.

JOHNNY: *(Looking at them)* It's hard to connect to them. I mean, I'm not the type who should have scarry hands.

FRANKIE: You're so good with knives. I've watched you.

JOHNNY: She admits it. The haughty waitress has cast a lustful gaze on the Knight of the Grill.

FRANKIE: "Can that new guy chop and dice," Dena tells me. "Look at him go."

JOHNNY: Now, sure! It's a breeze. I can dice an onion blindfolded. These scars were then. On my way up the culinary ladder. I knew you were looking at me.

FRANKIE: It's human curiosity. A new face in the kitchen. Male. Look, I never said I was a nun.

JOHNNY: Hey, it's okay. It was mutual. I was looking at you.

FRANKIE: Besides, there aren't that many short order cooks who have a dictionary and a copy of Shakespeare in their locker.

JOHNNY: You'd be surprised. We're an inquiring breed. We have our own quiz show: *Cooks Want to Know.*

FRANKIE: The one before you, Pluto, I'm not kidding, he said his name was Pluto, I swear to God! you know what he would have done with your books? Cooked 'em!

JOHNNY: So you noticed what I was reading, too?

FRANKIE: Call me the Bionic Eye. I don't miss a trick.

JOHNNY: You know what I liked about you? The way you take the time to talk to that old guy who comes in every day about three-thirty.

FRANKIE: Mr. Leon.

JOHNNY: With the cane and a copy of the *Post* and always has a flower in his lapel. You really are nice with him.

FRANKIE: He's really nice with me.

JOHNNY: You really talk to him. I also like the way you

fluff up that thing you wear on your uniform. It looks like a big napkin.

FRANKIE: It's supposed to be a handkerchief.

JOHNNY: I like the way you're always fluffing at it.

FRANKIE: What are you? Spying on me from the kitchen?

JOHNNY: Not spying. Watching.

FRANKIE: I'm going to be very self-conscious from now on.

JOHNNY: Watching and liking what I see.

FRANKIE: You in night school or something?

JOHNNY: This is my kind of night school.

FRANKIE: I meant the Shakespeare and the big words.

JOHNNY: I'm doing that on my own.

FRANKIE: Why?

JOHNNY: You don't want to be going out with a semi-illiterate, subcretinous, protomoronic asshole do you?

FRANKIE: Listen, it's easy to use words I don't know.

JOHNNY: What? Asshole? God, I like you.

FRANKIE: You still want a sandwich before you go?

JOHNNY: I still want a sandwich.

FRANKIE: Then you're going. You're not staying over.

JOHNNY: We'll cross that bridge when we get to it.

FRANKIE: There's no bridge to cross.

JOHNNY: What are you scared of?

FRANKIE: I'm not scared. *(She has resumed making sandwiches.* JOHNNY*watches her intently)* I'm not scared. I'm . . .

JOHNNY: Yes, you are.

FRANKIE: Well, not like in a horror movie. I don't think you're going to pull out a knife and stab me, if that's what you mean. Could we change the subject?

JOHNNY: What do you mean?

FRANKIE: Oh come on! You're gonna stand there and tell me you're not weird?

JOHNNY: Of course I'm weird.

FRANKIE: There's a whole other side of you I never saw at work.

JOHNNY: You thought all I did was cook?

FRANKIE: There's a whole other side of you I never saw when we were doing it either.

JOHNNY: It was probably your first experience with a passionate, imaginative lover.

FRANKIE: My first experience with an animal is more like it.

JOHNNY: Did you ever see an animal do to another animal's toes what I did to yours?

FRANKIE: Will you keep your voice down?

JOHNNY: You got this place bugged?

FRANKIE: I'm sure the whole building heard you. Ooooo! Ooooo! Ooooo!

JOHNNY: What do you expect, the way you kept twirling your fingers around inside my ears?

FRANKIE: Nobody ever put their fingers in your ears before?

JOHNNY: Maybe for a second but not the way you did, like you were drilling for something. I thought to myself, "Maybe she gets off on putting her fingers in guys' ears." But did I say anything? Did I call you weird?

FRANKIE: You should have said something.

JOHNNY: Why?

FRANKIE: I would have stopped.

JOHNNY: Are you crazy? I loved it. I'll try anything once, especially in that department. You got any new ideas? Keep 'em coming, keep 'em coming. I'll tell you when to stop.

FRANKIE: I can just hear you now at work: "Hey, guys, that Frankie put her fingers in your ears!"

JOHNNY: That is probably just about the last thing in the entire world I would ever do about tonight: talk about it to anyone, especially those animals at work. You really don't know me.

FRANKIE: It wouldn't be the first time one of you guys had yak-yak-yakked about it.

JOHNNY: Women yak, too. Hey, no catsup!

FRANKIE: Yeah, but about dumb things.

JOHNNY: All yakking is dumb. "I slept with Frankie." "Oh yeah, well I slept with Nancy Reagan." "Big effing pardon-my-French deal, the two of yous. I slept with Mother Teresa." So it goes. This wall of disparity between us, Frankie, we gotta break it down. So the only space left between us is just us.

FRANKIE: Here's your sandwich.

JOHNNY: Here's my guts.

FRANKIE: I'm sorry. I'm not good at small talk.

JOHNNY: This isn't small talk. This is enormous talk.

FRANKIE: Whatever you call it, I'm not good at it.

JOHNNY: Sure you are. You just have to want to be.

FRANKIE: Maybe that's it. I forgot the milk.

JOHNNY: Something's going on in this room, something important. You don't feel it?

FRANKIE: I told you what I felt.

JOHNNY: You don't want to feel it. Two people coming together: sure, it's a little scarey but it's pardon-my-French-again fucking wonderful, too. My heart is so full right now. Put your hand here. I swear to God, you can feel the lump. Go on, touch it.

FRANKIE: You're too needy. You want too much. I can't.

JOHNNY: That's where you're wrong.

FRANKIE: You had the whole thing. There's no more where it came from. I'm empty.

JOHNNY: I know that feeling. It's terrible. The wonderful thing is, it doesn't have to last.

FRANKIE: Turn the light off! I want to show you something. (JOHNNY *turns off the light*) Down one floor, over two buildings, the window with the kind of gauzy curtains. You see? *(JOHNNY has joined her at the window)*

JOHNNY: Where?

FRANKIE: There!

JOHNNY: The old couple in the bathrobes? What about 'em?

FRANKIE: I've been watching them ever since I moved in. Almost eight years now. I have never seen them speak to one another, not once. He'll sit there reading the paper and she'll cook an entire meal without him looking up. They'll eat it in total silence. He'll help her wash up sometimes but they still won't say a word. After a while the lights go out and I guess they've gone to bed.

(JOHNNY has seen something else out the window)

JOHNNY: Jesus!

FRANKIE: Those two! The Raging Bull, I call him. She's Mary the Masochist. They moved in about eighteen months ago.

JOHNNY: Hey!

FRANKIE: It's their thing.

JOHNNY: He's beating the shit out of her.

FRANKIE: She loves it.

JOHNNY: Nobody could love getting hit like that. We ought to do something.

FRANKIE: I saw her in the A&P. She was wearing a nurse's uniform. Living with him, that was a smart career choice. She had on sunglasses, you know, to hide the bruises. I went up to her, I figured it was now or never, and I said, "I live in the building behind you. I've seen how he hits you. Is there anything I can do?" and she just looked at me and said, "I don't know what you're talking about."

JOHNNY: Jesus, Jesus, Jesus.

FRANKIE: Some nights when there's nothing on television, I sit here in the dark and watch them. Once I ate a whole bunch of grapes watching them. One night she ended up on the floor and didn't move till the next morning. I hate being used to them.

JOHNNY: I would never hit you. I would never hit a woman.

FRANKIE: I think you had better finish that and go.

JOHNNY: You are missing one hell of an opportunity to feel with your own hand the human heart. It's right here.

FRANKIE: Maybe next time. (JOHNNY *looks at her and then downs the glass of milk in one long mighty gulp*) Thank you.

JOHNNY: Your meat loaf is directly from Mt. Olympus. Your father was a very lucky guy.

FRANKIE: It's his recipe. He taught me.

JOHNNY: Yeah? My old man was a great cook, too.

FRANKIE: Mine didn't have much choice.

JOHNNY: How do you mean?

FRANKIE: My mother left us when I was seven.

JOHNNY: I don't believe it! My mother left us when I was seven.

FRANKIE: Oh come on!

JOHNNY: Boy, you really, really, really and truly don't know me. Just about the last thing in the entire world I would joke about is a mother who wasn't there. I don't think mothers are sacred. I just don't think they're especially funny.

FRANKIE: Me and my big mouth! I don't think you realize how serious I am about wanting you to leave now.

JOHNNY: I don't think you realize how serious I am about us.

FRANKIE: What us? There is no us.

JOHNNY: I'm working on it. Frankie and Johnny! We're already a couple.

FRANKIE: Going out with someone just because his name is Johnny and yours is Frankie is not enough of a reason.

JOHNNY: I think it's an extraordinary one. It's fate. You also said you thought I had sexy wrists.

FRANKIE: One of the biggest mistakes in my entire life!

JOHNNY: It's gotta begin somewhere. A name, a wrist, a toe.

FRANKIE: Didn't they end up killing each other?

JOHNNY: She killed him. The odds are in your favor. Besides, we're not talking about ending up. I'm just trying to continue what's been begun.

FRANKIE: If he was anything like you, no wonder she shot him.

JOHNNY: It was a crime of passion. They were the last of the red hot lovers. We're the next.

FRANKIE: You're not from Brooklyn.

JOHNNY: Brooklyn Heights.

FRANKIE: I knew you were gonna say that! You're from outer space.

JOHNNY: Allentown, Pennsylvania, actually.

FRANKIE: Very funny, very funny.

JOHNNY: You've never been to Allentown.

FRANKIE: Who told you? Viv? Martin? I know, Molly the Mouth!

JOHNNY: Now who's from outer space? What the pardon-my-French fuck are you talking about?

FRANKIE: One of them told you I was from Allentown so now you're pretending you are so you can continue with this coincidence theory.

JOHNNY: You're from Allentown? I was born in Allentown.

FRANKIE: Very funny. Very funny.

JOHNNY: St. Stephen's Hospital. We lived on Martell Street.

FRANKIE: I suppose you went to Moody High School, too.

JOHNNY: No, we moved when I was eight. I started out at Park Lane Elementary though. Did you go to Park Lane? This is incredible! This is better than anything in Shirley MacClaine.

FRANKIE: It's a small world and Allentown's a big city.

JOHNNY: Not that small and not that big.

FRANKIE: I still don't believe you.

JOHNNY: Of course you don't. It's one big pardon-my-French-again fucking miracle and you don't believe in them.

FRANKIE: I'll tell you one thing: I could never, not in a million years, be seriously involved with a man who said "Pardon my French" all the time.

JOHNNY: Done. Finished. You got it.

FRANKIE: I mean, where do you pick up an expression like that?

JOHNNY: Out of respect for a person. A woman in this case.

FRANKIE: The first time you said it tonight I practically told you I had a headache and had to go home.

JOHNNY: That's so scary to me! That three little words, "Pardon my French," could separate two people from saying the three little words that make them connect!

FRANKIE: What three little words?

JOHNNY: I love you.

FRANKIE: Oh. Them. I should've guessed.

JOHNNY: Did you ever say them to anyone?

FRANKIE: Say them or mean them? My father, my first true love and a couple of thousand men since. That's about it.

JOHNNY: I'm not counting.

FRANKIE: You're really from Allentown? *(JOHNNY nods, takes a bite out of his sandwich and makes a "Cross My Heart" sign over his chest. Then he pushes his empty milk glass towards FRANKIE meaning he would like a refill, which she will get)* How did you get so lucky to get out of there at eight?

JOHNNY: *(Talking and eating)* My mother. She ran off with somebody she'd met at an AA meeting. My father took us to Baltimore. He had a sister. She couldn't cope with us. We ended up in foster homes. Could I have a little salt? I bounced all over the place. Washington, D.C., was the best. You go through that Smithsonian Institute they got there and there ain't nothing they're gonna teach you in college! That place is a goldmine. Portland, Maine, is nice, too. Cold though.

FRANKIE: You didn't miss much not staying in Allentown . . . My big highlight was . . .

JOHNNY: What?

FRANKIE: Nothing. It's stupid.

JOHNNY: I've told you stupid things.

FRANKIE: Not this stupid.

JOHNNY: No fair.

FRANKIE: All right! I played Fiona in our high school production of *Brigadoon*.

JOHNNY: What's stupid about that? I bet you were wonderful.

FRANKIE: It's hardly like winning a scholarship to Harvard or being the class valedictorian. It's an event; it shouldn't be a highlight.

JOHNNY: So you're an actress!

FRANKIE: You mean at this very moment in time?

JOHNNY: I said to myself, "She's not just a waitress."

FRANKIE: Yeah, she's an unsuccessful actress! What are you really?

JOHNNY: I'm really a cook.

FRANKIE: Oh. When you put it like that, I'm really a waitress. I haven't tried to get an acting job since the day I decided I never was gonna get one. Somebody told me you gotta have balls to be a great actress. I got balls, I told 'em. No, Frankie you got a big mouth!

JOHNNY: Would you . . . ? You know . . . ?

FRANKIE: What?

JOHNNY: Act something for me.

FRANKIE: What are you? Nuts? You think actors go around acting for people just like that? Like we do requests?

JOHNNY: I'm sorry. I didn't know.

FRANKIE: Acting is an art. It's a responsibility. It's a privilege.

JOHNNY: And I bet you're good at it.

FRANKIE: And it looks like I'll die with my secret. Anyway, what happened to your mother?

JOHNNY: I tracked her down when I was eighteen. They were still together, living in Philadelphia and both drinking again. They say Philadelphia will do that to you.

FRANKIE: So you saw her again? You see, I never did.

JOHNNY: But how this pot-bellied, balding, gin-breathed stranger could have been the object of anyone's desire but especially my mother's! She was still so beautiful, even through the booze, but he was a hundred percent turkey.

FRANKIE: Mine was killed in a car wreck about three,

no, four years ago. She was with her turkey. He got
it, too. I didn't hear about it for almost a month.

JOHNNY: What people see in one another! It's a total
mystery. Shakespeare said it best: "There are more
things in heaven and on earth than are dreamt of
in your philosophy, Horatio." Something like that.
I'm pretty close. Did you ever read *Hamlet?*

FRANKIE: Probably.

JOHNNY: I like him. I've only read a couple of his
things. They're not easy. Lots of old words.
Archaic, you know? Then all of a sudden he puts it
all together and comes up with something clear
and simple and it's real nice and you feel you've
learned something. This Horatio was Hamlet's best
friend. He thought he had it all figured out, so
Hamlet set him straight. Do you have a best
friend?

FRANKIE: Not really.

JOHNNY: That's okay. I'll be your best friend.

FRANKIE: You think a lot of yourself, don't you?

JOHNNY: Look, I'm going all over the place with you.
I might as well come right out with it: I love you.
I'm in love with you. I personally think we should
get married and I definitely want us to have kids,
three or four. There! That wasn't so difficult. You
don't have to say anything. I just wanted to get it
out on the table. Talk about a load off!

FRANKIE: Talk about a load off? Talk about a crock of shit.

JOHNNY: Hey, come on, don't. One of the things I like about you, Frankie, is that you talk nice. Don't start that stuff now.

FRANKIE: Well, fuck you how I talk! I'll talk any fucking way I fucking feel like it! It's my fucking apartment in the fucking first place and who the fuck are you to come in here and start telling me I talk nice. *(She has started to cry)*

JOHNNY: I'm sorry.

FRANKIE: Out of the blue, just like that, you've decided we're going to get involved?

JOHNNY: If you want to understate it like that.

FRANKIE: Whatever happened to a second date?

JOHNNY: We were beyond that two hours ago.

FRANKIE: Maybe you were.

JOHNNY: I like your apartment. That's a nice robe. You're a very pretty woman but I guess all the guys tell you that. Is that what you want?

FRANKIE: I don't want this.

JOHNNY: That has occurred to me. Dumb, I am not. Nervy and persistent, those I plead guilty to. I'm also something else people aren't too accustomed to these days: courageous. I want you and I'm coming after you.

FRANKIE: Has it occurred to you that maybe I don't want you?

JOHNNY: Only a couple of hundred times. I got my work cut out for me.

FRANKIE: Just because you take me out to dinner—!

JOHNNY: That wasn't my fault!

FRANKIE: Then the movies—!

JOHNNY: It got four stars!

FRANKIE: And end up making love—!

JOHNNY: Great love.

FRANKIE: Okay love.

JOHNNY: Great love. The dinner and the movie were lousy. We were dynamite.

FRANKIE: Okay, good love. So why do you have to go spoil everything?

JOHNNY: I told you I loved you. That makes me unlovable?

FRANKIE: It makes you a creep!

JOHNNY: Oh.

FRANKIE: No, I take that back. You're not a creep. You're sincere. That's what's so awful. Well, I'm sincere, too. I sincerely do not want to continue this.

JOHNNY: Pretend that we're the only two people in the entire world, that's what I'm doing, and it all falls into place.

FRANKIE: And I was looking forward to seeing you again.

JOHNNY: I'm right here.

FRANKIE: "God," I was thinking, "make him want to see me again without him knowing that's what I want."

JOHNNY: I already did know. God had nothing to do with it.

FRANKIE: I said, "See you again," not the stuff you're talking about. Kids, for Christ's sake!

JOHNNY: What's wrong with kids?

FRANKIE: I hate kids.

JOHNNY: I don't believe that.

FRANKIE: I'm too old to have kids.

JOHNNY: No, you're not.

FRANKIE: I can't have any. Now are you happy?

JOHNNY: We'll adopt.

FRANKIE: You just don't decide to fall in love with people out of the blue.

JOHNNY: Why not?

FRANKIE: They don't like it. How would you like it if Helen came up to you and said, "I'm in love with you. I want to have your baby."

JOHNNY: Who's Helen?

FRANKIE: At work.

JOHNNY: That Helen?

FRANKIE: You'd run like hell.

JOHNNY: She's close to seventy.

FRANKIE: I thought love was blind.

JOHNNY: It's the exact opposite. Besides, I'd tell her I was in love with you.

FRANKIE: You don't know me.

JOHNNY: Is that what all this is about? Of course I

don't know you. You don't know me either. We got off to a great start. Why do you want to stop?

FRANKIE: Does it have to be tonight?

JOHNNY: Yes!

FRANKIE: Who says?

JOHNNY: We may not make it to tomorrow. I might get knifed if you make me go home. You might choke on a chicken bone. Unknown poison gases could kill us both in our sleep. When it comes to love, life's cheap and it's short. So don't fuck with it and don't pardon my French.

FRANKIE: This is worse than *Looking for Mr. Goodbar.*

JOHNNY: Look, Frankie, I might see someone on the BMT tonight, get lucky and get laid, and think I was in love with her. This is the only chance we have to really come together, I'm convinced of it. People are given one moment to connect. Not two, not three, one! They don't take it, it's gone forever and they end up not only pardon-my-French-for-the-very-last-time screwing that person on the BMT but marrying her.

FRANKIE: Boy, are you barking up the wrong tree.

JOHNNY: I never thought I could be in love with a woman who said "barking up the wrong tree."

FRANKIE: You've driven me to it. I never used that expression in my entire life.

JOHNNY: You sure you don't want to feel this lump?

FRANKIE: Why won't you go?

JOHNNY: The only difference between us right now is I know how this is going to end—happily—and you don't. I need a best friend, too. Could I trouble you for another glass of milk?

FRANKIE: Okay, milk, but then I really want you to go. Promise?

JOHNNY: You drive a hard bargain. Milk for exile from the Magic Kingdom.

FRANKIE: Promise?

JOHNNY: Promise.

FRANKIE: Say it like you mean it.

JOHNNY: I promise.

FRANKIE: It's a good thing you're not an actor.

JOHNNY: All right, I don't promise.

FRANKIE: Now I believe you. *(She goes to the refrigerator and pours a glass of milk)*

Kathy Bates

Kenneth Welsh and Kathy Bate

Kathy Bates

JOHNNY: It's just words. It's all words. Words, words, words. He said that, too, I think. I read somewhere Shakespeare said just about everything. I'll tell you one thing he didn't say: I love you, Frankie.

(FRANKIE *brings him a glass of milk*)

FRANKIE: Drink your milk.

JOHNNY: I bet that's something else he never said: "Drink your milk," *The Merry Wives of Windsor,* Act Three, scene two. I don't think so. The Swan of Avon ain't got nothing on us.

FRANKIE: Did anybody ever tell you you talk too much?

JOHNNY: Yeah, I told you about half an hour ago. There's no virtue in being a mute.

FRANKIE: I'm not a mute.

JOHNNY: Did I say you were?

FRANKIE: I talk when I have something to say.

JOHNNY: Did I say she was a mute?

FRANKIE: You know, not everybody thinks life is a picnic. Some of us have problems. Some of us have sorrows. But people like you are so busy telling us what you want, how you feel, you don't even notice the rest of us who aren't exactly jumping up and down for joy.

JOHNNY: I haven't done anything but notice you.

FRANKIE: Shut up!

JOHNNY: Who's jumping up and down!

FRANKIE: I said, shut up! Just drink your milk and go. I don't want to hear your voice again tonight.

JOHNNY: What do you want?

FRANKIE: I want to be alone. I want to watch television. I want to eat ice cream. I want to sleep. I want to stop worrying I'm trapped in my own apartment with a fucking maniac.

JOHNNY: We all have problems, you know.

FRANKIE: Right now, mine begin and end with you. You said you'd go.

JOHNNY: I lied.

FRANKIE: All I have to do is open that window and start screaming.

JOHNNY: In this city? Lots of luck.

FRANKIE: I have neighbors upstairs, friends . . .

JOHNNY: No one's gonna want to get involved in us. They'll just tell you to call the police.

FRANKIE: Don't think it hasn't crossed my mind.

JOHNNY: They'll come, give or take an hour or two. They'll make me leave but I'll be right back. That's a very handy fire escape. If not tonight, then tomorrow or the day after that. Sooner or later, you're gonna have to deal with me. Why don't we just get it over with? Besides, tomorrow's Sunday. We can sleep in.

(At some point before this, the music on the radio has changed to Scriabin's Second Symphony. Neither FRANKIE *nor* JOHNNY *heard the announcement. Ideally, the audience didn't either)*

FRANKIE: I *am* trapped in my own apartment with a fucking maniac!

JOHNNY: You don't mean that. I'm trying to improve my life and I'm running out of time. I'm still going around in circles with you. There's gotta be that one thing I say that makes you listen. That makes us connect. What station are you on?

FRANKIE: What?

JOHNNY: It looks like it's around about ninety. You got a paper? *(He starts rummaging about for a newspaper)*

FRANKIE: What do you think you're doing?

JOHNNY: I want to get the name of that piece of music you liked for you.

FRANKIE: I don't care anymore.

JOHNNY: Well, I do. When you come across something beautiful, you gotta go for it. It doesn't grow on trees, beautiful things. *(He has found the radio station call letters in the newspaper)* WKCC. *(As he dials information)* I owe you a quarter.

FRANKIE: He's nuts. Out and out loco!

JOHNNY: *(Into phone)* Give me the number for WKCC. Thank you. *(To FRANKIE)* Without the name, we'll lose that music and I'll never find it on my own. You let something like that slip through your fingers and you deserve rock and roll! *(He hangs up and immediately redials)* I hate these recordings that give you the number now. One less human contact. *(To FRANKIE)* Where are you going?

FRANKIE: Out and you better not be here when I get back.

JOHNNY: You want to pick up some Haagen-Dazs Vanilla Swiss Almond while you're out?

FRANKIE: I said get out! *(She starts throwing things)* You're a maniac! You're a creep! You're a . . . Oh!

JOHNNY: *(Into phone)* May I speak to your disc jockey? . . . Well, excuse me! *(He covers phone, to FRANKIE)* They don't have a disc jockey. They have someone called Midnight with Marlon. *(Into phone)* Hello, Marlon? My name is Johnny. My friend and I were making love and in the afterglow, which I sometimes think is the most beautiful part of making love, she noticed that you were playing some really beautiful music, piano. She was right. I don't know much about quality music, which I could gather that was, so I would like to know the name of that particular piece and the artist performing it so I can buy the record and present it to my lady love, whose name is Frankie and is that a beautiful coincidence or is it not? *(Short pause)* Bach. Johann Sebastian, right? I heard of him. The *Goldberg Variations.* Glenn Gould. Columbia Records. *(To* FRANKIE*)* You gonna remember this? *(*FRANKIE *smacks him hard across the cheek.* JOHNNY *takes the phone from his ear and holds it against his chest. He just looks at her. She smacks him again. This time he catches her hand while it is still against his cheek, holds it a beat, then brings it to his lips and kisses it. Then, into phone, he continues but what he says is really for* FRANKIE, *his eyes never leaving her)* Do you take requests, Marlon? Then make an exception! There's a man and a woman. Not young, not old. No great beauties, either one. They meet where they work: a restaurant and it's not the Ritz. She's a waitress. He's a cook. They meet but they don't connect. "I got two medium burgers working" and "Pick up, side of fries" is pretty much the extent of it. But she's noticed him, he can feel it. And he's noticed her. Right off. They both knew tonight was going to happen. So why did it take him six weeks for him to ask her if she wanted to see a movie that neither one of them could tell you the name of right now? Why did they eat ice cream sundaes before she asked him if he wanted to come up since they were in the neighborhood? And then

they were making love and for maybe an hour they
forgot the ten million things that made them think,
"I don't love this person. I don't even like them,"
and instead all they knew was that they were together and it was perfect and they were perfect
and that's all there was to know about it and as they
lay there, they both began the million reasons not
to love one another like a familiar rosary. Only this
time he stopped himself. Maybe it was the music
you were playing. They both heard it. Only now
they're both beginning to forget they did. So
would you play something for Frankie and Johnny
on the eve of something that ought to last, not self-
destruct. I guess I want you to play the most beautiful music ever written and dedicate it to us. *(He
hangs up)* Don't go.

FRANKIE: Why are you doing this?

JOHNNY: I'm tired of looking. Everything I want is in
this room.

(He kisses her. FRANKIE *responds. It quickly gets passionate.* FRANKIE *starts to undress)*

JOHNNY: Let me.

FRANKIE: Hunh?

JOHNNY: Let me do it. *(He helps her out of her rain-
coat. Then he takes it and hangs it up.* FRANKIE
*stands a little awkwardly in the center of the room
waiting for him to come back to her)* Make yourself

at home. That was a little joke. No, that was a little bad joke. *(He turns off a lamp)*

FRANKIE: What's the matter?

JOHNNY: Nothing.

FRANKIE: Leave the lights on.

JOHNNY: It's better off.

FRANKIE: I want to see you this time.

(JOHNNY has started unbuttoning her blouse)

JOHNNY: I don't like to make love with the lights on.

FRANKIE: Why not?

JOHNNY: I can't.

FRANKIE: That's a good reason.

(JOHNNY is having a little difficulty undressing her)

JOHNNY: It's because of Archie.

FRANKIE: Okay, I'll bite. Who's Archie?

JOHNNY: A huge Great Dane at one of my foster families. I mean, massive. Whenever I'd jack off, he'd just stare at me. At it. Talk about serious castration anxiety! So I got in the habit of doing it with the lights off.

FRANKIE: Sometimes I am so glad I'm a girl.

JOHNNY: I'm also a romantic. I think everything looks better in half-light and shadows.

FRANKIE: That's not romance, that's hiding something. Romance is seeing somebody for what they really are and still wanting them warts and all.

JOHNNY: I got plenty of them. *(He stops undressing her)* I'm forty-five.

FRANKIE: You look younger. I'm thirty-seven.

JOHNNY: So do you. I'm forty-six.

FRANKIE: Honest?

JOHNNY: I'll be forty-eight the tenth of next month.

FRANKIE: What do you want for your birthday?

JOHNNY: To be able to stop bullshitting about things like my age.

FRANKIE: I'll be thirty-nine on the eleventh.

JOHNNY: We're both what-do-you-ma-call-its!

FRANKIE: Figures! Gimme a hand with the bed. I hate it when the sheets get like that. *(FRANKIE starts straightening up the bed. JOHNNY turns off another light in the room before helping her to smooth the sheets and blankets)* I'm the one who

ought to be hiding from the light. Me and my goddamn inverted nipples. I hate the way they look.

JOHNNY: Don't be silly.

FRANKIE: Yeah? You be a woman and have someone
invert your nipples and see how you like it.

JOHNNY: I love your nipples.

FRANKIE: Well, I hate 'em.

JOHNNY: What do you know? *(They stand on opposite
sides of the bed shaking out the sheets)* Listen, I
wish I was circumcised.

FRANKIE: Sounds like you had your chance and blew
it.

JOHNNY: Hunh?

FRANKIE: The dog. Skip it, skip it! I'll be forty-one on
the eleventh.

JOHNNY: Big deal. So what do you want?

FRANKIE: The same thing you do and a new pair of
tits.

JOHNNY: Hey, it means a lot to me you talk nice.
*(*JOHNNY *crosses to window to close the shade.*
FRANKIE *goes to bed and lies down on it)* Jesus. *(He
points to something outside the window and above
it)*

FRANKIE: Come away from there. It's not good for you.

JOHNNY: Come here. Quick. *(He stands at the window. Moonlight covers his body)*

FRANKIE: I mean it. I've looked too long.

JOHNNY: There's a full moon! You can just see it between the buildings. Will you look at that! Now that's what I call beautiful!

FRANKIE: I ordered it just for you. Macy's. Twenty-five bucks an hour.

JOHNNY: Look at it!

FRANKIE: Later.

JOHNNY: It won't be there later.

(FRANKIE joins him at the window)

JOHNNY: You can almost see it move.

FRANKIE: *(Lowering her gaze)* All quiet on the Western front. For now. Come on. *(She moves to bed)* Come on. I want you to make love to me.

(JOHNNY turns from the window)

JOHNNY: I want to make love to you.

FRANKIE: Woof! Woof! *(Nothing)* It was a joke, I'm sorry.

RADIO ANNOUNCER: This young man was very persuasive . . .

JOHNNY: Ssshh! Listen! *(He moves quickly to the bedside radio and turns up the volume)*

RADIO ANNOUNCER: So although it's against my policy to play requests, there's an exception to every rule. I don't know if this is the most beautiful music ever written, Frankie and Johnny—and how I wish that really were your names but I know when my leg is being pulled—but whoever you are, where ever you are, whatever you're doing, I hope this is something like what you had in mind.

(Debussy's "Clair de Lune" is heard. JOHNNY *switches off the bedside lamp and kisses* FRANKIE. *Then he gets up quickly, goes to the window and reaches for the shade. He sees the two couples in the apartments across the courtyard. He looks up to the moon. There is moonlight spilling onto his face and body. He decides not to pull the shade, allowing the moonlight to spill into the room. He moves away from the window and disappears in the shadows of the bed. We hear a distant siren. We hear the Debussy. We hear the sounds of* FRANKIE *and* JOHNNY *starting to make love. Fifteen seconds of this. Abrupt silence. Total blackout)*

END OF ACT I

ACT II

ACT II

AT RISE: *The only illumination in the room comes from the television set. In its gray light, we can see Frankie and Johnny in the bed, under the covers. They both stare at it.*

The only sound is coming from the radio: now it is playing "The Ride of the Walkyries." Thirty seconds of the Wagner.

JOHNNY: Is that Charles Bronson? *(JOHNNY turns down radio)* Is that Charles Bronson?

FRANKIE: Or the other one. I always get people in those kinds of movies confused.

JOHNNY: James Coburn?

FRANKIE: I think that's his name.

JOHNNY: Whoever he is, I hate him. It's not Clint Eastwood?

FRANKIE: No. I know what Clint Eastwood looks like. Look, you don't have to make such a big deal about it.

JOHNNY: I'm not making a big deal about it.

FRANKIE: Then how come we stopped?

JOHNNY: I haven't stopped. We're taking a little break. Will you look at that! I am appalled at the violence in the world today.

FRANKIE: It's okay if we don't.

JOHNNY: I know.

FRANKIE: Really.

JOHNNY: I said I know. Jesus, he drove a fucking nail through his head!

FRANKIE: I had my eyes shut.

JOHNNY: And when did that asshole go from playing our song to those screaming mimis? I thought he liked us. That kind of music is bad enough during normal hours. But when you're trying to make love to someone . . . ! Talk about not knowing how to segue from one mood to the next! I ought to call that station and complain. *(We hear him trip over something)* Goddamnit!

(FRANKIE turns on the bedside lamp)

FRANKIE: Are you all right?

JOHNNY: I wish you wouldn't leave— Yeah. Since I'm up, you want something?

FRANKIE: Johnny.

JOHNNY: You're the one who's making a big deal about it. I'm fine. I'm not upset. Look, I'm dancing. Now yes or no? What do you want?

FRANKIE: A Western on white down and a glass of milk.

JOHNNY: Very funny. What do you want? A beer? *(We can see him in the light of the open refrigerator as he searches it for food and drink)*

FRANKIE: I want a Western and a glass of milk.

JOHNNY: We're in the middle of something. This is a little rest, not a major food break. Besides, you just ate.

FRANKIE: I'm still hungry.

JOHNNY: I'm opening you a beer.

FRANKIE: I want a Western and a glass of milk.

JOHNNY: I never know when you're kidding me or not. I think that's one of the things I like about you but I'm not sure.

FRANKIE: I'm not kidding you. I'm starving and what I would like is one of your Westerns and a glass of milk. Everyone says you make a great Western.

JOHNNY: They do?

FRANKIE: So come on, Johnny, Johnny . . . ravish me with your cooking.

JOHNNY: You mean, since I couldn't ravish you with my body?

FRANKIE: No, that's not what I mean.

JOHNNY: Look, this is a temporary hiatus. I would like to keep it that way.

FRANKIE: So would I. I'll eat fast.

JOHNNY: All I'm saying is that if we get into real food now and I start cooking you a Western and chopping onions and peppers, it's going to be very hard to get back into the mood for what we were doing and which, contrary to your impression perhaps, I was enjoying enormously. All I asked for was a little breather, for Christ's sake!

FRANKIE: I only asked for a sandwich.

JOHNNY: You asked for a Western. Westerns mean chopping and dicing and sautéing and . . . you know what goes into a Western! Come on, Frankie, it's not like you asked for a peanut butter and jelly on a Ritz cracker. You want food food.

FRANKIE: I suppose I could call out.

JOHNNY: All right, all right! *(He starts getting ingredients out of the refrigerator and slamming them onto the work counter)* I just wish somebody would tell me how we got from a mini-sex problem to a major pig-out.

FRANKIE: I don't think there's a connection.

JOHNNY: I wasn't going to tell you this but since

you're not sparing my feelings, I'm not going to go on sparing yours: this is the first time anything like this ever happened to me.

FRANKIE: So?

JOHNNY: Well, if you can't make the connection . . . !

FRANKIE: Between what and what?

JOHNNY: It takes two to tango.

FRANKIE: You mean it's my fault you conked out?

JOHNNY: I didn't say it was anybody's fault. And I didn't conk out. I'm resting.

FRANKIE: Oh, the old And-on-the-Seventh-Day Syndrome!

JOHNNY: There's no need to be sarcastic.

FRANKIE: Then don't blame me your dancing dog didn't dance when you told it to. That sounds terrible. Don't blame me for your limp dick. Now what about my Western?

JOHNNY: You expect me to make you a sandwich after that?

FRANKIE: After what?

JOHNNY: Insulting my manhood.

FRANKIE: I didn't insult your manhood. I merely described a phase it was going through. Everything has phases. To talk about the new moon doesn't insult the old one. You have a lovely manhood. It's just in eclipse right now so you can make me one of your terrific Westerns.

JOHNNY: This is the first time this has ever happened to me. I swear to God.

FRANKIE: I believe you.

JOHNNY: I hate it. I hate it a lot.

FRANKIE: Just be glad you have someone as sympathetic as me to share it with.

JOHNNY: Don't make fun.

FRANKIE: I'm not. *(She goes to him and comforts him)* It's okay.

JOHNNY: You're lucky women don't have problems like this.

FRANKIE: We've got enough of our own in that department.

JOHNNY: It's male menopause. I've been dreading this.

FRANKIE: You know what I think it was? The moonlight. You were standing in it. It was bathing your body. I've always been very suspicious of what moonlight does to people.

JOHNNY: It's supposed to make them romantic.

FRANKIE: Or turn you into a werewolf. That's what I was raised on. My grandmother was always coming into my bedroom to make sure the blinds were down. She was convinced sleeping in the moonlight would turn you into the wolfman. I thought if I slept in the moonlight I'd wake up a beautiful fairy princess, so I kept falling asleep with the blinds open and she kept coming in and closing them. She always denied it was her. "Wasn't me, precious. Must have been your Guardian Angel." Remember them?

JOHNNY: What do you mean, "remember"?

FRANKIE: One night I decided to stay awake and catch her in the act. It seemed like forever. When you're that age, you don't have anything to stay awake *about.* So you're failing geography, so what? Finally my grandmother came into the room. She had to lean across my bed to close the blinds. Her bosom was so close to my face. She smelled so nice. I pretended I was still sleeping and took the deepest breath of her I could. In that one moment, I think I knew what it was like to be loved. Really loved. I was so safe, so protected! That's better than being pretty. I'll never forget it. The next thing I knew it was morning and I still didn't look like Audrey Hepburn. Now when I lie in bed with the blinds up and the moonlight spilling in, I'm not

thinking I want to be somebody else, I just want
my Nana back.

JOHNNY: Nana? You called your grandmother Nana?
That's what I called mine.

FRANKIE: It's not that unusual.

JOHNNY: It's incredible! I don't know anybody else
who called their grandmother Nana. I always
thought it was very unusual of me and more than
anything else I wanted to be like everyone else.

FRANKIE: You, like everyone else?

JOHNNY: It was a disaster. "Why do we call her
Nana?" I used to ask my mother—this was before
Philadelphia—"Everyone else says Grandma."
"We just do," she told me. My mother was not one
for great answers. Sort of a Sphinx in that department. Anyway, I for one am very glad you didn't
wake up Audrey Hepburn. She's too thin. People
should have meat on their bones. "Beware yon
Cassius. He hath a lean and hungry look."

FRANKIE: Who's Cassius?

JOHNNY: I don't know. But obviously he was thin and
Shakespeare thinks we should be wary of skinny
people.

FRANKIE: Why?

JOHNNY: Well, you know how they are. Grim. Kind of waiting and watching you all the time.

FRANKIE: Like Connie?

JOHNNY: Who?

FRANKIE: Connie Cantwell. She works weekends. Red hair, wears a hairnet?

JOHNNY: Exactly! Wouldn't you beware her?

FRANKIE: I've actually seen her steal tips.

JOHNNY: There you go! He's filled with little tips like that. "Neither a borrower nor a lender be."

FRANKIE: That's just common sense. You don't have to be a genius to figure that one out.

JOHNNY: Of course not. But he put it in poetry so that people would know up here what they already knew in here and so they would remember it. "To be or not to be."

FRANKIE: Everyone knows that. Do I want to kill myself?

JOHNNY: Well?

FRANKIE: Well, what?

JOHNNY: Do you want to kill yourself?

FRANKIE: Of course not. Well, not right now. Everybody wants to kill themself some of the time.

JOHNNY: They shouldn't.

FRANKIE: Well, they do! That doesn't mean they're gonna do it. Could we get off this?

JOHNNY: The list just gets longer and longer.

FRANKIE: What list?

JOHNNY: The us list, things we got in common.

FRANKIE: What do you want to kill yourself about some times?

JOHNNY: Right now? My limp dick. I'm kidding, I'm kidding. I'm going to start warning you before I say something funny.

FRANKIE: You don't have to warn me. Just say something funny.

JOHNNY: I want to kill myself sometimes when I think I'm the only person in the world and the part of me that feels that way is trapped inside this body that only bumps into other bodies without ever connecting with the only other person in the world trapped inside of them. We gotta connect. We just have to. Or we die.

FRANKIE: We're connecting.

JOHNNY: Are we?

FRANKIE: I am. I feel very . . .

JOHNNY: Say it.

FRANKIE: I don't know what it is.

JOHNNY: Say it anyway.

FRANKIE: Protective, but that's crazy!

JOHNNY: It's nice.

FRANKIE: I'm looking for somebody to take care of me this time.

JOHNNY: We all are.

FRANKIE: Why do we keep going from one subject I don't like to another?

JOHNNY: We're like an FM station when you're out driving in a car. We keep drifting and we gotta tune ourselves back in.

FRANKIE: Who says?

JOHNNY: Hey, I'm being nice.

FRANKIE: May I say something without you biting my head off?

JOHNNY: Aw, c'mon!

FRANKIE: I mean it!

JOHNNY: You are the woman I've been looking for all my adult life. You can say anything you want. Speak, queen of my heart, speak!

FRANKIE: That's just what I was talking about.

JOHNNY: What? Queen of my heart?

FRANKIE: I'm not the queen of anybody's heart.

JOHNNY: Fine. So what is it?

FRANKIE: This is going to sound awfully small potatoes now.

JOHNNY: You couldn't speak in small potatoes if you wanted to.

FRANKIE: I still want a Western.

JOHNNY: You don't give up. You're like a rat terrier with a bone.

FRANKIE: I'm sorry.

JOHNNY: I didn't hear that.

FRANKIE: All right, I'm *not* sorry. I'm a very simple person. I get hungry and I want to eat.

JOHNNY: I'm also a very simple person.

FRANKIE: Sure you are!

JOHNNY: I see something I want, I don't take no. I used to but not anymore.

FRANKIE: What is that supposed to mean?

JOHNNY: My life was happening to me. Now I'm making it happen. Same as with you and this sandwich. You wanted it, went for it and won. *(He turns and opens the refrigerator)* You can tell a lot about someone from what they keep in their ice box. That and their medicine chest. I would've made a terrific detective.

FRANKIE: Just stay out of my medicine chest. And I didn't appreciate you going through my purse either.

JOHNNY: Someone is clearly not prepared for the eruption into her what-she-thinks-is-humdrum life of an extraordinary man, chef and fellow worker. Why don't you try our friend on the radio again? *(FRANKIE will go to radio and turn it on)* Personally, I think it was all his fault. When it comes to music, I'm a mellow sort of guy. That last thing he played was for people playing with themselves, not one another. "If music be the food of love, play on." You-Know-Who.

FRANKIE: *(At the radio)* I would love a cigarette.

JOHNNY: Over my dead body.

FRANKIE: That doesn't mean I'm going to smoke one. *(She turns up volume. We hear the César Franck Sonata for Piano and Violin.)* How's that?

JOHNNY: *Comme ci, comme ça.*

FRANKIE: It's pretty.

JOHNNY: Let's put it this way: he's no Bach. The first thing in the morning, I'm going to buy you those *Goldberg Variations.*

FRANKIE: It's Sunday. Everything'll be closed.

JOHNNY: Monday then.

FRANKIE: I guess Bach was Jewish. The *Goldberg Variations.*

JOHNNY: I read somewhere a lot of great composers were.

FRANKIE: I thought you were Jewish.

JOHNNY: In New York, that's a good assumption.

FRANKIE: I just realized I don't know your last name.

JOHNNY: I don't know yours.

FRANKIE: Mine's right on the bell. It's all over this place.

JOHNNY: We don't need last names. We're Frankie

and Johnny. *(Closing the refrigerator door)* Boy, you just shot my ice box theory all to hell. You should be an Irish longshoreman from what you've got in there.

FRANKIE: I am. Had you fooled for a while there, didn't I?

(JOHNNY is getting ready to make the Western)

JOHNNY: Now watch how I do this. After this, you're on your own!

(JOHNNY begins to work with the food and the utensils. He works swiftly, precisely and with great elan. He is a virtuoso in the kitchen. FRANKIE will pull up a stool and watch him work)

FRANKIE: I know I'm going to regret saying this but I thought I was the only person I knew who referred to one of those things as an ice box.

JOHNNY: Now who's pulling whose leg?

FRANKIE: And I don't say things like phonograph or record player. Just "ice box" and I only dimly remember us having one when I was about that big.

JOHNNY: Do you know what the population of New York City is?

FRANKIE: Eight million?

JOHNNY: Nine million, six hundred eighty-four thousand, four hundred eleven. Exactly two of them refer to those things as ice boxes. Those two, after you-know-what-ing their brains out, are now engaged in making a Western sandwich somewhere in Hell's Kitchen.

FRANKIE: It's Clinton actually.

JOHNNY: You still gonna call that a coincidence? Boy, I bet the Swan of Avon would have had something to say about that!

FRANKIE: I believe there's a reason for everything and I like to know what it is. One and one are two.

JOHNNY: That's mathematics. We're talking people.

FRANKIE: One and one should be two with them, too. Too many people throw you a curve nowadays and you end up with a three.

JOHNNY: Do I hear the voice of bitter experience?

FRANKIE: I wasn't born yesterday, if that's what you're talking about. *(She has watched* JOHNNY *intently during this as he has continued to prepare the Western)* That's something I've never seen anyone do.

JOHNNY: What?

FRANKIE: Chop the pepper that fine.

JOHNNY: 'Cause they're looking for short cuts.

FRANKIE: You're incredible with that knife.

JOHNNY: Thank you.

FRANKIE: And don't say it's all in the wrists.

JOHNNY: It is.

FRANKIE: I hate that expression. It's such a "fuck you." What people really mean is "I know how to do it and you don't. Ha ha ha!"

JOHNNY: What brought that on? We're talking nice and Bingo! the armor goes up.

FRANKIE: What about your armor?

JOHNNY: I don't have any.

FRANKIE: Everybody has armor. They'd be dead if they didn't.

JOHNNY: Bloody but unbowed.

FRANKIE: Besides, I wasn't talking about you.

JOHNNY: Where's your cayenne?

FRANKIE: I don't have any. I don't even know what it is. What's that you just put in?

JOHNNY: Wouldn't you like to know? *(He does a good imitation of* FRANKIE*)* "Ha ha ha!"

FRANKIE: C'm'on!

JOHNNY: Salt, just salt!

FRANKIE: Is that all?

JOHNNY: Cooking's no big deal.

FRANKIE: It is if you can't.

JOHNNY: You just never had anyone to cook for. The way I feel about you I feel a Duck à l'Orange Flambée with a puree of water chestnuts coming on!

FRANKIE: I like food. I just never saw the joy in cooking it. My mother hated cooking. Her primary utensil was a can opener. I even think she resented serving us on plates. She used to eat right out the pots and pans. "One less thing to clean. Who's to know? We ain't got company."

JOHNNY: This isn't the right kind of bread.

FRANKIE: Gee, I'll run right out!

JOHNNY: There you go again! You want a good Western down, you need the right bread.

FRANKIE: Did you always want to be a cook?

JOHNNY: About as much as you wanted to be a waitress.

FRANKIE: That bad, hunh?

JOHNNY: When I look at some of the choices I made
with my life, it seems almost inevitable I would
end up slinging hash.

FRANKIE: Same with me and waitressing. I was supposed to graduate high school and work for a second cousin who had a dental laboratory.

JOHNNY: That place down by the old train station?

FRANKIE: Yeah, that's the one.

JOHNNY: His son was in my class. Arnold, right?

FRANKIE: You knew my cousin Arnold?

JOHNNY: Enough to say hello. Finish your story.

FRANKIE: Anyway, they made bridges, plates, retain-
ers, stuff like that there. A dentist would take a
parafin impression of the patient's mouth and
make plaster of Paris molds for the technicians to
work from.

JOHNNY: No wonder the acting bug bit.

FRANKIE: I never had what it takes. I hope I have
what it takes to be something but I know it's not an
actress. You know what I'm thinking about?

JOHNNY: What?

FRANKIE: You won't laugh?

JOHNNY: Of course not.

FRANKIE: I can't. It's too . . . I'll tell you later. I can't now.

JOHNNY: Okay. I'll tell you one thing. You didn't miss much not graduating high school. I had almost two years of college. We both ended up working for a couple of crazed Greeks. *(He imitates their boss)* "Cheeseburger, cheeseburger" is right.

FRANKIE: That was very good.

JOHNNY: Thank you.

FRANKIE: A teacher.

JOHNNY: Hunh?

FRANKIE: What I'm thinking of becoming.

JOHNNY: Why would I laugh at that?

FRANKIE: I don't know. It just seems funny. Someone who can't spell "cat" teaching little kids to. I'll have to go back to school and learn before I can teach them but . . . I don't know, it sounds nice. *(She hasn't stopped watching* JOHNNY *work with the eggs)* Aren't you going to scramble them?

JOHNNY: It's better if you just let them set.

FRANKIE: In the restaurant, I've seen you beat 'em. That's when I noticed you had sexy wrists.

JOHNNY: That's in the restaurant: I'm in a hurry. These are my special eggs for you. *(He starts cleaning up while the eggs set in a skillet on the stove top)*

FRANKIE: You don't have to do that.

JOHNNY: I know.

FRANKIE: Suit yourself.

JOHNNY: I bet I know what you're thinking: "He's too good to be true."

FRANKIE: Is that what you want me to think?

JOHNNY: Face it, Frankie, men like me do not grow on trees. Hell, *people* like me don't. *(He holds his wet hands out to her)* Towel? *(FRANKIE picks up a dish towel on the counter and begins to dry his hands for him)* So you think I have sexy wrists?

FRANKIE: I don't think you're gonna break into movies on 'em.

JOHNNY: What do you think is sexy about them?

FRANKIE: I don't know. The shape. The hairs. That vein there. What's that?

JOHNNY: A mole.

FRANKIE: I could live without that.

JOHNNY: First thing Monday morning, it comes off.

(He is kissing her hands. FRANKIE *lets him but keeps a certain distance, too)*

FRANKIE: Are you keeping some big secret from me?

JOHNNY: It's more like I'm keeping several thousand little ones.

FRANKIE: I'd appreciate a straight answer.

JOHNNY: No, I'm not married.

FRANKIE: Men always think that's the only question women want to ask.

JOHNNY: So fire away.

FRANKIE: Well, were you?

JOHNNY: I was.

FRANKIE: How many times?

JOHNNY: Once. Is that it?

FRANKIE: Men have other secrets than being married. You could be a mass murderer or an ex-convict.

JOHNNY: I am. I spent two years in the slammer. Forgery.

FRANKIE: That's okay.

JOHNNY: The state of New Jersey didn't seem to think so.

FRANKIE: It's no skin off my nose.

JOHNNY: Anything else?

FRANKIE: You could be gay.

JOHNNY: Get real, Frankie.

FRANKIE: Well, you could!

JOHNNY: Does this look like a gay face?

FRANKIE: You could have a drug problem or a drinking one.

JOHNNY: All right, I did.

FRANKIE: Which one?

JOHNNY: Booze.

FRANKIE: There, you see?

JOHNNY: It's under control now.

FRANKIE: You could still be a real shit underneath all that.

JOHNNY: But I'm not.

FRANKIE: That's your opinion.

JOHNNY: You just want a guarantee we're going to live happily ever after.

FRANKIE: Jesus, God knows, I want something. If I was put on this planet to haul hamburgers and french fries to pay the rent on an apartment I don't even like in the vague hope that some stranger will not find me wanting enough not to want to marry me then I think my being born is an experience that is going to be equaled in meaninglessness only by my being dead. I got a whole life ahead of me to feel like this? Excuse me, who do I thank for all this? I think the eggs are ready.

JOHNNY: Everything you said, anybody could say. I could give it back to you in spades. You didn't invent negativity.

FRANKIE: I didn't have to.

JOHNNY: And you didn't discover despair. I was there a long time before you ever heard of it.

FRANKIE: The eggs are burning.

JOHNNY: Fuck the eggs! This is more important!

FRANKIE: I'm hungry!

(FRANKIE *has gone to stove to take the eggs off.* JOHNNY *grabs her from behind and pulls her toward him)*

JOHNNY: What's the matter with you?

FRANKIE: Let go of me!

JOHNNY: Look at me! *(They struggle briefly.* FRANKIE *shoves* JOHNNY, *who backs into the hot skillet and burns his back)* Aaaaaaaaaaaaaaa!

FRANKIE: What's the matter—?

JOHNNY: Oooooooooooooo!

FRANKIE: What happened—?

JOHNNY: Ow! Ow! Ow! Ow! Ow! Ow! Ow!

FRANKIE: Oh my God!

JOHNNY: Oooo! Oooo! Oooo! Ooooo! Oooo! Oooooo!

FRANKIE: I'm sorry, I didn't mean to—!

JOHNNY: Jesus, Frankie, Jesus Christ!

FRANKIE: Tell me what to do!

JOHNNY: Get something!

FRANKIE: What?

JOHNNY: Ice.

FRANKIE: Ice for burns? Don't move.

(FRANKIE *puts the entire tray of ice cubes on* JOHN-NY*'s back. The scream that ensues is greater than the first one)*

JOHNNY:
AAAAAAAAAAAAAAAAAAAAAAAAAAAAA!!!!!!!!!!

FRANKIE: You said to—! *(*JOHNNY *nods vigorously)* Should I keep it on? *(*JOHNNY *nods again, only this time he bites his fingers to keep from crying out)* We'd be a terrific couple. One of us would be dead by the end of the first week. One date practically did it. All I asked you to do was turn off the eggs but no! everything has to be a big deal with you. I would have made the world's worst nurse.

JOHNNY: *(Between gasps of pain)* Butter.

FRANKIE: What?

JOHNNY: Put some butter on it.

FRANKIE: Butter's bad on burns.

JOHNNY: I don't care.

FRANKIE: I may have some . . . oh what-do-you-call-it-when-you-have-a-sunburn, it comes in a squat blue bottle?

JOHNNY: Noxzema!

FRANKIE: That's it!

JOHNNY: It breaks me out. Get the butter.

FRANKIE: It's margarine.

JOHNNY: I don't care.

(FRANKIE *gets the margarine out of the refrigerator*)

FRANKIE: It sounds like you got a lot of allergies.

JOHNNY: Just those three.

FRANKIE: Catsup, Noxzema and . . . what was the other one?

JOHNNY: Fresh peaches. Canned are okay. (FRANKIE *puts the margarine on* JOHNNY's *back*) Oooooooooooo!

FRANKIE: Does that feel good?

JOHNNY: You have no idea.

FRANKIE: More?

JOHNNY: Yes, more. Don't stop.

FRANKIE: You're gonna smell like a . . . whatever a person covered in margarine smells like.

JOHNNY: I don't care.

FRANKIE: To tell the truth, it doesn't look all that bad.

JOHNNY: You think I'm faking this?

FRANKIE: I didn't say that.

JOHNNY: What do you want? Permanent scars?

(Pause. FRANKIE *puts more margarine on* JOHNNY's *back)*

FRANKIE: Did your first wife do this for you?

JOHNNY: Only wife. I told you that.

FRANKIE: Okay, so I was fishing.

JOHNNY: No, checking. Were you married?

FRANKIE: No, never.

JOHNNY: Anyone serious?

FRANKIE: Try "terminal."

JOHNNY: What happened?

FRANKIE: He got more serious with who I thought was my best friend.

JOHNNY: The same thing happened to me.

FRANKIE: You know what the main thing I felt was? Dumb.

JOHNNY: I know, I know!

FRANKIE: I even introduced them. I lent them money. Money from my credit union. I gave her my old television. A perfectly good Zenith. They're probably watching Charles Bronson together at this very moment. I hope it explodes and blows their faces off. No, I don't. I hope it blows up and the fumes kill them. Aren't there supposed to be poison gases in a television set?

JOHNNY: I wouldn't be surprised.

FRANKIE: That or he's telling her she looks like shit, who told her she could change her hair or where's his car keys or shut the fuck up, he's had a rough day. I didn't know how exhausting unemployment could be. God, why do we get involved with people it turns out hate us?

JOHNNY: Because . . .

FRANKIE: . . . we hate ourselves. I know. I read the same book.

JOHNNY: How long has it been?

FRANKIE: Seven years. *(JOHNNY lets out a long stream of air)* What? You, too? *(JOHNNY nods)* Any kids?

JOHNNY: Two.

FRANKIE: You see them?

JOHNNY: Not as much as I'd like. She's remarried. They live in Maine in a beautiful house overlooking the sea.

FRANKIE: I bet it's not so beautiful.

JOHNNY: It's beautiful. I could never have provided them with anything like that. The first time I saw it, I couldn't get out of the car. I felt so ashamed. So forgotten. The kids came running out of the house. They looked so happy to see me but I couldn't feel happy back. All of a sudden, they looked like somebody else's kids. I couldn't even roll down the window. "What's the matter, Daddy?" I started crying. I couldn't stop. Sheila and her husband had to come out of the house to get me to come in. You know what I wanted to do? Run that crewcut asshole insurance salesman over and drive off with the three of them. I don't know where we would've gone. We'd probably still be driving.

FRANKIE: That would've been a dumb thing to do.

JOHNNY: I never said I was smart.

FRANKIE: I'll tell you a secret: you are.

JOHNNY: I said I was passionate. I don't let go of old things easy and I grab new things hard.

FRANKIE: Too hard.

JOHNNY: There's no such thing as too hard when you want something.

FRANKIE: Yes, there is, Johnny. The other person.

(There is a pause. FRANKIE *has stopped working on* JOHNNY's *back. Instead, she just stares at it.* JOHNNY *looks straight ahead. The music has changed to the Shostakovich Second String Quartet)*

JOHNNY: What are you doing back there?

FRANKIE: Nothing. You want more butter or ice or something?

*(*JOHNNY *shakes his head)*

JOHNNY: It's funny how you can talk to people better sometimes when you're not looking at them. You're right there. *(He points straight ahead)* Clear as day.

FRANKIE: I bet no one ever said this was the most beautiful music ever written.

JOHNNY: I don't mind.

FRANKIE: I don't know what the radio was doing on that station in the first place. That's not my kind of music. But I could tell you were enjoying it and I guess I wanted you to think I had higher taste than I really do.

JOHNNY: So did I.

FRANKIE: I liked what he played for us though, but he didn't say its name.

JOHNNY: Maybe it doesn't need one. You just walk into a fancy record shop and ask for the most beautiful music ever written and that's what they hand you.

FRANKIE: Not if I was the salesperson. You'd get "Michelle" or "Eleanor Rigby" or "Lucy in the Sky with Diamonds." Something by the Beatles. I sort of lost interest in pop music when they stopped singing.

JOHNNY: The last record I bought was the Simon and Garfunkel Reunion in Central Park. It wasn't the same. You could tell they'd been separated.

FRANKIE: Sometimes I feel like it's still the sixties. Or that they were ten or fifteen years ago, not twenty or twenty-five. I lost ten years of my life somewhere. I went to Bruce Springsteen last year and I was the oldest one there.

JOHNNY: Put your arms around me. (FRANKIE *puts her arms over* JOHNNY's *shoulders*) Tighter. (FRANKIE's *hands begin to stroke* JOHNNY's *chest and stomach*) Do you like doing that?

FRANKIE: I don't mind.

JOHNNY: We touch our own bodies there and nothing happens. Something to do with electrons. We short-circuit ourselves. Stroke my tits. There! *(He tilts his head back until he is looking up at her)* Give me your mouth. (FRANKIE *bends over and kisses him. It is a long one)* That tongue. Those lips. *(He pulls her down toward him for another long kiss)* I want to die like this. Drown.

FRANKIE: What do you want from me?

JOHNNY: Everything. Your heart. Your soul. Your tits. Your mouth. Your fucking guts. I want it all. I want to be inside you. Don't hold back.

FRANKIE: I'm not holding back.

JOHNNY: Let go. I'll catch you.

FRANKIE: I'm right here.

JOHNNY: I want more. I need more.

FRANKIE: If I'd known what playing with your tit was gonna turn into—

JOHNNY: Quit screwing with me, Frankie.

FRANKIE: You got a pretty weird notion of who's screwing with who. I said I liked you. I told you that. I'm perfectly ready to make love to you. Why do you have to start a big discussion about it. It's not like I am saying "no."

JOHNNY: I want you to do something.

FRANKIE: What?

JOHNNY: I want you to go down on me.

FRANKIE: No.

JOHNNY: I went down on you.

FRANKIE: That was different.

JOHNNY: How?

FRANKIE: That was then.

JOHNNY: Please.

FRANKIE: I'm not good at it.

JOHNNY: Hey, this isn't a contest. We're talking about making love.

FRANKIE: I don't want to right now.

JOHNNY: You want me to go down on you again?

FRANKIE: If I do it, will you shut up about all this other stuff?

JOHNNY: You know I won't.

FRANKIE: Then go down on yourself.

JOHNNY: What happened? You were gonna do it.

FRANKIE: Anything to get you to quit picking at me. Go on, get out of here. Get somebody else to go down on you.

JOHNNY: I don't want somebody else to go down on me.

FRANKIE: Jesus! I just had a vision of what it's going to be like at work Monday after this! I'm not quitting my job. I was there first.

JOHNNY: What are you talking about?

FRANKIE: I don't think we're looking for the same thing.

JOHNNY: We are. Only I've found it and you've given up.

FRANKIE: Yes! Long before the sun ever rose on your ugly face.

JOHNNY: What scares you more? Marriage or kids?

FRANKIE: I'm not scared. And I told you: I can't have any.

JOHNNY: I told you: we can adopt.

FRANKIE: I don't love you.

JOHNNY: That wasn't the question.

FRANKIE: You hear what *you* want to hear.

JOHNNY: Do you know anybody who doesn't?

FRANKIE: Not all the time.

JOHNNY: You're only telling me you don't love me so you don't have to find out if you could. Just because you've given up on the possibility, I'm not going to let you drag me down with you. You're coming up to my level if I have to pull you by the hair.

FRANKIE: I'm not going anywhere with a man who for all his bullshit about marriage and kids and Shakespeare . . .

JOHNNY: It's not bullshit!

FRANKIE: . . . just wants me to go down on him.

JOHNNY: Pretend it was a metaphor.

FRANKIE: Fuck you it was a metaphor! It was a blow job. What's a metaphor?

JOHNNY: Something that stands for something else.

FRANKIE: I was right the first time. A blow job.

JOHNNY: A sensual metaphor for mutual acceptance.

FRANKIE: Fuck you. Besides, what's mutual about a blow job.

JOHNNY: I made that up. I'm sorry. It wasn't a metaphor. It was just something I wanted us to do.

FRANKIE: And I didn't.

JOHNNY: Let go, will you! One lousy little pecadillo and it's off with his head!

FRANKIE: Stop using words I don't know. What's a pecadillo?

JOHNNY: A blow job! Notice I haven't died you didn't do it!

FRANKIE: I noticed.

JOHNNY: And let me notice something for you: you wouldn't have died if you had. Thanks for making me feel about this big. *(He gets up and starts gathering and putting on his clothes)* I'm sorry, I mistook you for a kindred spirit. Kindred: two of a kind, sharing a great affinity.

FRANKIE: I know what kindred means!

JOHNNY: Shall we go for affinity!

FRANKIE: That's the first really rotten thing you've said all night. Somebody who would make fun of somebody else's intelligence, no worse, their education or lack of—that is somebody I would be very glad not to know. I thought you were weird, Johnny. I thought you were sad. I didn't think you were cruel.

JOHNNY: I'm sorry.

FRANKIE: It's a cruelty just waiting to happen again and I don't want to be there when it does.

JOHNNY: Please! *(There is an urgency in his voice that startles* FRANKIE*)* I'm not good with people. But I want to be. I can get away with it for long stretches but I always hang myself in the end.

FRANKIE: Hey, c'm'on, don't cry. Please, don't cry.

JOHNNY: It's not cruelty. It's a feeling I don't matter. That nobody hears me. I'm drowning. I'm trying to swim back to shore but there's this tremendous undertow and I'm not getting anywhere. My arms and legs are going a mile a minute but they aren't taking me any closer to where I want to be.

FRANKIE: Where's that?

JOHNNY: With you.

FRANKIE: You don't know me.

JOHNNY: Yes, I do. It scares people how much we really know one another, so we pretend we don't. You know me. You've known me all your life. Only now I'm here. Take me. Use me. Try me. There's a reason we're called Frankie and Johnny.

FRANKIE: There's a million other Frankies out there
and a billion other Johnnys. The world is filled with
Frankies and Johnnys and Jacks and Jills.

JOHNNY: But only one this Johnny, one this Frankie.

FRANKIE: We're too different.

JOHNNY: You say po-tah-toes? All right, I'll say po-tah-
toes! I don't care. I love you. I want to marry you.

FRANKIE: I don't say po-tah-toes. Who the hell says
po-tah-toes?

JOHNNY: Are you listening to me?

FRANKIE: I'm trying very hard not to!

JOHNNY: That's your trouble. You don't want to hear
anything you don't think you already know. Well,
I'll tell you something, Cinderella: Your Prince
Charming has come. Wake up before another thousand years go by! Don't throw me away like a gum
wrapper because you think there's something
about me you may not like. I have what it takes to
give you anything and everything you want.
Maybe not up here . . . *(He taps his head)* . . .
or here . . . *(He slaps his hip where he wears his
wallet)* . . . but here. And that would please me
enormously. All I ask back is that you use your
capacity to be everyone and everything for me. It's
within you. If we could do that for each other we'd
give our kids the universe. They'd be Shakespeare
and the most beautiful music ever written and a

saint maybe or a champion athlete or a president all rolled into one. Terrific kids! How could they not be. We have a chance to make everything turn out all right again. Turn our back on everything that went wrong. We can begin right now and all over again but only if we begin right now, this minute, this room and us. I know this thing, Frankie.

FRANKIE: I want to show you something, Johnny. *(She pushes her hair back)* He did that. The man I told you about. With a belt buckle.

(JOHNNY kisses the scar)

JOHNNY: It's gone now.

FRANKIE: It'll never go.

JOHNNY: It's gone. I made it go.

FRANKIE: What are you? My guardian angel?

JOHNNY: It seems to me the right people are our guardian angels.

FRANKIE: I wanted things, too, you know.

JOHNNY: I know.

FRANKIE: A man, a family, kids . . . He's the reason I can't have any.

JOHNNY: He's gone. Choose me. Hurry up. It's getting light out. I turn into a pumpkin.

FRANKIE: *(Looking toward the window)* It is getting light out! *(She goes to the window)*

JOHNNY: You are so beautiful standing there.

FRANKIE: The only time I saw the sun come up with a guy was my senior prom. *(JOHNNY has joined her at the window. As they stand there looking out, we will be aware of the rising sun)* His name was Johnny Di Corso but everyone called him Skunk. *(She takes JOHNNY's hand and clasps it to her but her eyes stay looking out the window at the dawn)* He was a head shorter than me and wasn't much to look at but nobody else had asked me. It was him or else. I was dreading it. But guess what? That boy could dance! You should have seen us. We were the stars of the prom. We did lindys, the mambo, the twist. The monkey, the frug. All the fast dances. Everybody's mouth was down to here. Afterwards we went out to the lake to watch the sun come up. He told me he was going to be on "American Bandstand" one day. I wonder if he ever made it.

(JOHNNY puts his arm around her and begins to move her in a slow dance step)

JOHNNY: There must be something about you and sunrises and men called Johnny.

FRANKIE: You got a nickname?

JOHNNY: No. You got to be really popular or really unpopular to have a nickname.

FRANKIE: I'll give you a nickname. *(They dance in silence awhile. Silence, that is, except for the Shostakovich, which they pay no attention to)* You're not going to like me saying this but you're a terrible dancer.

JOHNNY: Show me.

FRANKIE: Like that.

JOHNNY: There?

FRANKIE: That's better.

JOHNNY: You're going to make a wonderful teacher. *(He starts to hum)*

FRANKIE: What's that supposed to be?

JOHNNY: Something from *Brigadoon.*

FRANKIE: That isn't from *Brigadoon.* That isn't even remotely from *Brigadoon.* That isn't even remotely something from anything. *(They dance.* FRANKIE *begins to hum)* That's something from *Brigadoon.* You can't have kids in a place this size.

JOHNNY: Who says?

FRANKIE: How big is your place?

JOHNNY: Even smaller. We'll be a nice snug family. It'll be wonderful.

FRANKIE: Does it always get light so fast this time of year?

JOHNNY: Unh-unh. The sun's in a hurry to shine on us.

FRANKIE: Pardon my French but that's bullshit.

JOHNNY: You can sleep all day today.

FRANKIE: What are you planning to do?

JOHNNY: Watch you.

FRANKIE: You're just weird enough to do it, too. Well, forget it. I can't sleep with people watching me.

JOHNNY: How do you know?

FRANKIE: I was in the hospital for my gall bladder and I had a roommate who just stared at me all the time. I made them move me. I got a private room for the price of a semi. Is this the sort of stuff you look forward to finding out about me?

JOHNNY: Unh-hunh!

FRANKIE: You're nuts.

JOHNNY: I'm happy!

FRANKIE: Where are you taking me?

JOHNNY: The moon.

FRANKIE: That old place again?

JOHNNY: The other side this time.

(JOHNNY has slow-danced FRANKIE to the bed. The room is being quickly flooded with sunlight)

FRANKIE: If you don't turn into a pumpkin, what do you turn into?

JOHNNY: You tell me. *(He kisses her very gently)*

FRANKIE: Just a minute.

(She gets up and moves quickly to the bathroom. JOHNNY turns off all the room lights. He starts to close the blinds but instead raises them even higher. Sunlight pours across him. The Shostakovich ends. JOHNNYmoves quickly to the radio and turns up the volume as the ANNOUNCER's VOICE is heard)

RADIO ANNOUNCER: . . . that just about winds up my stint in the control room. This has been "Music till Dawn with Marlon." I'm still thinking about Frankie and Johnny. God, how I wish you two really existed. Maybe I'm crazy but I'd still like to believe in love. Why the hell do you think I work these hours? Anyway, you two moonbeams, whoever, wherever you are, here's an encore.

(Debussy's "Clair de Lune" is heard again. JOHNNY *sits, listening. He starts to cry he is so happy. He turns as* FRANKIE *comes out of the bathroom. She is brushing her teeth)*

JOHNNY: They're playing our song again.

FRANKIE: Did they say what it was this time?

JOHNNY: I told you! You just walk into a record shop and ask for the most beautiful music . . .

FRANKIE: Watch us end up with something from *The Sound of Music,* you'll see! You want to brush? *(She motions with her thumb to the bathroom. She steps aside as* JOHNNY *passes her to go in)* Don't worry. It's never been used. *(Still brushing her teeth, she goes to the window and looks out)* Did you see the robins? *(She listens to the music)* This I can see why people call pretty. *(She sits on the bed, listens and continues to brush her teeth. A little gasp of pleasure escapes her)* Mmmmm!

*(*JOHNNY *comes out of the bathroom. He is brushing his teeth)*

JOHNNY: I'm not going to ask whose robe that is.

FRANKIE: Sshh! *(She is really listening to the music)*

JOHNNY: We should get something with fluoride.

FRANKIE: Sshh!

JOHNNY: Anti-tartar buildup, too.

FRANKIE: Johnny!

(JOHNNY *sits next to her on the bed. They are both brushing their teeth and listening to the music.*

They continue to brush their teeth and listen to the Debussy. The lights are fading)

END OF THE PLAY